SPORTS STARS WITH HEART

Peyton Manning

LEADER ON AND OFF THE FIELD

by Tim Polzer

Enslow Publishers, Inc.
40 Industrial Road
Box 398
Berkeley Heights, NJ 07922
USA
http://www.enslow.com

Library of Congress Cataloging-in-Publication Data
Polzer, Tim.
  Peyton Manning : leader on and off the field / Tim Polzer. — 1st ed.
      p. cm. — (Sports stars with heart)
  Includes bibliographical references and index.
  ISBN 0-7660-2822-4
  1. Manning, Peyton—Juvenile literature. 2. Football players—United
States—Biography—Juvenile literature. I. Title. II. Series.
  GV939.M289P493 2006
  796.332092—dc22
  [B]   2006012545

Credits
Editorial Direction: Red Line Editorial, Inc. (Bob Temple)
Editor: Sue Green
Designer: Lindaanne Donohoe

Printed in the United States of America

10 9 8 7 6 5 4 3 2 1

To Our Readers: We have done our best to make sure all Internet addresses in this book were active and appropriate when we went to press. However, the author and the publisher have no control over and assume no liability for the material available on those Internet sites or on other Web sites they may link to. Any comments or suggestions can be sent by e-mail to comments@enslow.com or to the address on the back cover.

Photographs © 2006: AP Photo/Scott Audette: 98; AP Photo/Ed Bailey: 35; AP Photo/Ed Betz: 37; AP Photo/Judi Bottoni: 43, 111; AP Photo/Michael Conroy: 4, 11, 67; AP Photo/Darron Cummings: 1, 3, 32; AP Photo/The Indianapolis Star, Matt Detrich: 108; AP Photo/file: 18, 22, 29; AP Photo/Mike Groll: 94; AP Photo/Mark Humphrey: 3, 53, 57; AP Photo/ Robert E. Klein: 104; AP Photo/Charles Krupa: 103; AP Photo/KD Lawson: 55; AP Photo/Adam Nadel: 64; AP Photo/AJ Mast: 3, 80, 101; AP Photo/Wade Payne: 25; AP Photo/Ed Reinke: 45, 49; AP Photo/Tom Strattman: 76, 85; AP Photo/Ron Schwane: 88

Cover Photo: Peyton Manning, quarterback of the Indianapolis Colts, calls a play in a game against the Green Bay Packers September 26, 2004.

C O N T E N T S

Indianapolis Colts quarterback Peyton Manning throws a pass.

CHAPTER ONE

Touchdown King

The day after Christmas 2004, Indianapolis Colts quarterback Peyton Manning made history and established himself as one of the NFL's all-time great passers.

With about a minute to play in regulation, the Colts trailed the San Diego Chargers 31–23, but Manning remained calm and collected. His hands did not shake. His mind did not wander. He was focused on the challenge he faced, and he was determined to lead his team from behind.

As the nearly 60,000 spectators who made up the Colts' home crowd rose to their feet, filling the RCA Dome with a loud roar, Manning confidently stepped into the huddle and looked his teammates in the eyes.

"People think I'm a numbers guy, but [for me] it's about winning."

—Peyton Manning

Despite the loud noise and tension, the Colts' offensive unit appeared focused on the quarterback. He and his teammates had spent many hours preparing for this moment. They had total confidence in Manning, and he had confidence in his teammates.

Manning called the play and the snap count and clapped his hands as the offense broke the huddle in unison. Stepping to the line of scrimmage, Manning paused to study the Chargers' defense and the 21 yards that stood between the Colts, the goal line, and their comeback try. The distance was shorter than many of his completed passes but now seemed like a very long way to go.

Manning reached beneath the center and barked out his signals. He took the football as it was snapped sharply into his hands. Clutching the seams of the football with his fingers, the quarterback stepped back, looking over the field for his receivers. It was a sequence he had performed thousands of times in his head since he was just a little boy.

At the end of his pass drop, Manning set his feet, maintaining a springy but balanced stance. Huge defensive linemen charged around him, pushing against the Colts' offensive linemen and trying to reach the quarterback before he could throw the ball. It was now time to find an open man.

Colts receiver Brandon Stokley, running a post pattern, sprinted forward before turning toward the center of the field. Hours of practicing pass routes with his pass catchers told Manning where each of his receiving targets would be on the field. He instantly saw Stokley was open.

In a split second, Manning shifted the football back from his right shoulder, stepped forward with his left foot, and threw the ball in a tight spiral. The ball zoomed past Chargers defenders and into the hands of Stokley. He never broke stride, racing into the end zone for a touchdown.

While the team celebrated the score, Manning looked to the Colts' sideline for the next play call. No one could tell by looking at Manning that he had just broken Dan Marino's single-season record for touchdown passes.

"People think I'm a numbers guy, but [for me] it's about winning," Manning said. [1]

ALL ABOUT THE GAME

The loud crowd cheered equally for the Colts' comeback and Manning's record-breaking touchdown pass, but the quarterback never paused. His team still had work to do if it was going to win the game and secure a number three seed in the playoffs. The Colts needed two more points to tie, or the day would be ruined.

On the two-point conversion try, Manning backpedaled as if he were going to pass. Instead, he handed the ball to running back Edgerrin James on a draw play. The play fooled the Chargers' defense as James ran across the goal line to tie the score at 31. Now Manning and the Colts had a chance to win the game in overtime.

The Colts' crowd continued to stand, clapping their hands and giving Manning an ovation for his performance. But the quarterback remained humble and focused on the job at hand. Even though Manning had broken a record that long seemed unbreakable, he thought more of his team than himself. He asked that the game not be stopped for a ceremony. He did not want a celebration to put the spotlight on him or hurt his team's chances for winning. If the Colts could win, there would be plenty of time to celebrate later.

This selfless show of sportsmanship did not seem unusual to Manning's

DID YOU KNOW?
Dan Marino congratulated Peyton Manning after his first NFL game. Even though the Dolphins beat the Colts, Marino was impressed that Manning passed for 302 yards.

teammates and coaches, who already knew how dedicated their quarterback was to the team and his performance on the football field.

Manning's focus on his team helped lead the Colts from behind that day. Forgetting the record for the moment, Manning quarterbacked the Colts on a 61-yard drive that ended with Mike Vanderjagt's game-winning 30-yard field goal in overtime.

Afterward, reporters wanted to know what Manning thought about his record-breaking performance. Instead of praising himself, he paid tribute to his teammates and another legendary Colts quarterback.

"The way it happened on that drive, I think Johnny Unitas would have been proud," he said of the NFL Hall of Famer considered one of the best quarterbacks ever to have played the game.

"At the time I threw it, there wasn't a lot of emotion for me, because if we don't get the two-point conversion, this is a down locker room right now," Manning said. "The fact that it happened, we won the game . . . it sure made for an exciting day."[2]

AN UNBEATABLE RECORD

Manning's exciting day turned back the clock twenty years to 1984 when Miami Dolphins quarterback Dan Marino set a seemingly incredible mark. In just his second year as a professional, Marino threw 48 touchdown passes while leading the Dolphins to the Super Bowl that season. He also became the first NFL player to pass for more than 5,000 yards in a season.

Marino's new record bettered the previous high of 36 touchdown passes held by both Y.A. Tittle and George Blanda. Marino would throw another 44 touchdown passes two seasons later. Before Peyton Manning challenged Marino's mark, the closest any other player got to Marino's record was Kurt Warner, who threw 41 touchdown passes with the St. Louis Rams in 1999.

Before retiring after the 1999 season, Marino would break career NFL records for attempts, completions, yards, and touchdowns. It's no wonder he was elected for induction to the Pro Football Hall of Fame in 2005.

Breaking Marino's record was far from Manning's mind as he entered the 2004 season. After losing to New England in the American Football Conference championship game the previous season, Manning set his efforts on leading the Colts to the playoffs and their first Super Bowl since 1971.

Manning was

PASSING QUOTE

When Dan Marino, then a television analyst for CBS, was asked how teams should deal with Peyton Manning's bid to break his single-season touchdown record, Marino said, "Blitz him!"

Manning is greeted by his father, Archie Manning.

coming off his personal best 99.0 quarterback rating in 2003. While leading the Colts to within one victory of the NFL's title game, he also became the first NFL quarterback to produce three games of five touchdowns or more in a season.

Manning's performance in 2003 was so good, many critics wondered if he could improve one season later. But he worked as hard as ever to improve his body and his knowledge during the off-season.

His dedication and hard work paid off when the 2004 NFL season began. He threw 9 touchdown passes in the Colts' first three games, including 5 against the Green Bay Packers in Week 3. But it wasn't until the Colts' eighth game that the NFL world began wondering if Manning might break

Marino's twenty-year-old record. That's when Manning produced an unbelievable hot streak.

In a five-game span, he threw another 5 touchdown passes against the Kansas City Chiefs, followed by 4 against the Minnesota Vikings, 5 more against the Houston Texans, 4 against the Chicago Bears, and 6 against the Detroit Lions. Manning totaled 24 touchdown passes—a number many quarterbacks do not reach in an entire sixteen-game season.

Week after week, reporters began questioning Manning about his chances of breaking Marino's record. He tried to make his team the story, but there was no doubt that the quarterback was close to making history. "I feel uncomfortable talking about anything individual," Manning said. "I just want to keep winning."[3]

When the Colts took the field against the Chargers, football fans across the globe watched as Manning entered the regular season's next-to-last game. He needed two touchdown passes to break Marino's benchmark. The record-breaking day began as one of the toughest of the season for Manning and his team. The Chargers' defense, determined not to be the victim of a new record, often confused him by disguising its pass coverages. The Chargers also mounted a heavy pass rush, sacking Manning 4 times and often pressuring him to hurry his passes before his receivers were open.

Despite the Chargers' tough play, Manning and the Colts did not give up or get discouraged. Manning had studied video of the Chargers' defense for many hours in preparation for the game. He kept trying to find weaknesses to let his teammates make plays.

Manning's homework paid off in the third quarter. He tied Marino's record with a 3-yard shovel pass to James Mungro before setting up the dramatic, record-breaking drive and play.

Late in the game, the scoreboard and the clock did not favor the Colts. But the skills and savvy of their quarterback gave them an advantage. With less than five minutes remaining in the game, the Chargers led. Manning found his team facing fourth down with 4 yards to go from his own 25-yard line.

He waved the Colts' punt team off the field. Punting the ball back to the Chargers would be safe but would leave the Colts little time to come back. He was confident his team could gain the 4 yards necessary for keeping their comeback drive alive. If he was right, the Colts had a

DID YOU KNOW?

After the game, both Peyton Manning and Brandon Stokley couldn't find the football used on Manning's record-breaking 49th touchdown pass.

It turned out that Pro Football Hall of Fame representatives took control of the ball after Stokley's catch.

The Colts kept the ball and display it in their team Hall of Fame.

better chance to win. If he was wrong, the Chargers would probably win the game.

Manning took the snap from center and connected with receiver Reggie Wayne for a 19-yard

PASSING MARINO
Here is a game-by-game breakdown of Peyton Manning's touchdown passes during his record-breaking 2004 season.

Week	Opponent	TD Passes
1	New England	2
2	Tennessee	2
3	Green Bay	5
4	Jacksonville	2
5	Oakland	3
6	Bye	0
7	Jacksonville	3
8	Kansas City	5
9	Minnesota	4
10	Houston	5
11	Chicago	4
12	Detroit	6
13	Tennessee	3
14	Houston	2
15	Baltimore	1
16	San Diego	2
17	Denver	0
Total		49

completion and a first down. The Colts' quarterback was on a roll. He then completed passes to tight end Dallas Clark and favorite receiver Marvin Harrison to move the Colts close enough for Stokley's touchdown and his place in the NFL record book.

Stokley, who caught the record-breaking touchdown pass, told reporters that Manning was a truly great quarterback—if not the greatest ever.

"He's the best that's ever played this game as far as quarterbacks are concerned," Stokley said. "When he's retired, they'll compare everybody to Peyton Manning, without a doubt."[4]

Manning won't be satisfied until the Colts win the Super Bowl. He wasn't satisfied after setting the NFL single-season touchdown pass record. When the 2004 season was done, he reflected on his performance, analyzing every game and every pass. When he was finished, he realized that he should have thrown even more touchdown passes.

Of all the Colts' offensive plays in 2004, Manning found 17 that should have produced touchdowns. The 17 incomplete passes were the result of a receiver dropping the ball or Manning making a poor throw.

Manning sets high standards for himself. He believes that he should have thrown 66 touchdown passes in 2004, rather than just 49.

CHAPTER TWO

Opening Night

Peyton Manning's introduction to football began soon after his birth on March 24, 1976. It's not surprising that he came to know and love football. Peyton's father, Archie Manning, was one of football's most famous quarterbacks in the seventies.

When Peyton was born, Archie was a five-year veteran quarterback of the New Orleans Saints. During their father's fourteen-year NFL career, Peyton and his brothers Cooper and Eli would grow up amidst the good and bad times that go with being an NFL quarterback.

The Manning boys inherited their father's love for sports. From an early age, Archie learned to play the sports offered in the small town of Drew, Mississippi.

"From as early as I can remember, I played every sport in school and on the playgrounds, which in

Drew meant four: football, basketball, baseball and track," Archie said.[1]

Archie wanted to follow in his own father's footsteps and play football for Drew High School. Archie soon proved to be an excellent quarterback. He quickly took a liking to the position.

> **DID YOU KNOW?**
> Peyton Manning was named after Archie's uncle Peyton who drove young Archie to watch Drew High School games in an old Studebaker car.

"I was quarterback from sixth grade on. The challenge of playing quarterback was as thrilling as it was daunting," Archie said. "The position is made to order for athletes who are natural leaders."[2]

Before leaving Drew High School, Archie attracted a football scholarship offer from the University of Mississippi in Oxford. But he faced a tough decision. He also was a star baseball player at Drew and had attracted the attention of pro scouts. Over the years,

> **DID YOU KNOW?**
> Archie Manning was a four-sport letterman at Drew High School, participating in football, baseball, basketball, and track.

he would be drafted by Atlanta, Kansas City, and the Chicago White Sox of Major League Baseball.

17

Ole Miss quarterback Archie Manning readies a pass in 1969.

Archie really wanted to play football, so he passed on a quick paycheck and trip to baseball's minor leagues to play football for Mississippi, also known as Ole Miss.

Freshmen did not play football in the Southeastern Conference, but Archie won the starting quarterback job as a sophomore. His hustle and quickness quickly made him a crowd favorite.

As an Ole Miss quarterback, Archie never won a national championship or even a Southeastern Conference crown. But his individual performances and his ability to lead the underdog Rebels to upsets against highly-ranked teams raised him to hero status.

Years later, when Peyton was seven or eight years old, a friend sent the Mannings a collection of audio broadcasts of Archie's Ole Miss games. Peyton played the tapes again and again. He loved to hear the Manning name called over the radio and dreamed of following in his father's football footsteps.

"I listened to those tapes over and over again, like I was hearing them for the first time," Peyton said. [3]

He liked to listen to one memorable game in particular. In the fall of 1969, Archie turned in one of the greatest games in NCAA history, passing for 436 yards and 3 touchdowns and rushing for 104 yards in a 33–32 loss to Alabama. The first nationally televised prime time college game to be broadcast across the country helped spread Archie's fame to a nation.

During his three seasons at Ole Miss, Archie led the Rebels to wins against three top-five teams, including a 38–0 victory against highly-ranked Tennessee. Archie finished fourth in voting for the 1969 Heisman Trophy and was named United Press International's Offensive Player of the Year. He finished third in the following year's Heisman Trophy contest.

When Archie left Ole Miss, he owned the school record for total career touchdown passes (56) for thirty years until his son Eli surpassed him with 86. Eli also bettered his father's 4,753 passing yards, but Archie still holds the Ole Miss record for rushing by a quarterback with 823 yards.

Archie's legacy at Ole Miss continues. The school retired his number 18 jersey and posted speed limit signs of 18 miles per hour on roads throughout the campus. Archie later was voted Mississippi's all-time greatest athlete. He even became the subject of a novelty song called "The Ballad of Archie Who." He later would be inducted into the College Football Hall of Fame.

DID YOU KNOW?

Peyton Manning's mother, Olivia, first saw her future husband, Archie, when his Drew High School basketball team upset her high school team from Philadelphia, Mississippi. Archie and Olivia didn't actually meet until a year later at Ole Miss.

It was at Ole Miss that Archie met his eventual wife and Peyton's mother, Olivia. She was voted the Ole Miss homecoming queen in their senior year. They were married in 1971, the same year Archie turned pro.

After a legendary college career, Archie was selected as the second overall pick of the 1971 NFL Draft by the New Orleans Saints. His college exploits and likeable personality made him an instant hero among the Saints' regional fans in Louisiana and bordering Mississippi.

Unfortunately, the Saints were not a very good team when they drafted Archie, four years after they had joined the NFL as an expansion team. He became the Saints' starting quarterback during his rookie season and improved quickly. He led the NFL with 448 passing attempts and 230 completions in his second season.

An exciting aspect of Archie's game was his running ability, which produced 18 rushing touchdowns, including 4 in 1971 and 5 in 1977.

It's a good thing that Archie was an elusive, scrambling quarterback. The Saints' offensive line was not very good. Archie spent a lot of time running away from rushing defenders. Quarterback sacks weren't tallied as an official statistic during Archie's NFL career, but he probably suffered more sacks than any quarterback in league history.

New Orleans quarterback Archie Manning scrambles for yardage November 19, 1978, in a game at Texas Stadium.

The effects of the physical beating Archie received each week caused him to struggle through many injuries. Tendinitis in his right shoulder kept him sidelined during the 1976 season.

Archie's quick feet and quick thinking were not enough to lift the struggling Saints. They never recorded a winning season during his eleven years with the team. As the team's best known player, he often became a target of critics who blamed him for the Saints' poor performances.

FOOTBALL AND FAMILY

Archie didn't let his team's losing habits or his aches and pains affect his time with his sons. He left his work behind when he came home to Cooper, Peyton, and Eli.

"There were a lot of days when he got beat up on the field and the Saints played badly, but he signed every autograph, he did every single interview and that's what it's all about," Peyton said. "He never brought his sorrows home, either. When he came home to the family, you'd thought he had just won the Super Bowl." [4]

The Manning brothers also witnessed some of the tough things that go along with being a professional athlete. They sometimes missed their father

DID YOU KNOW?

When Saints fans began wearing "Aints" paper bags over their heads at games, Peyton and older brother, Cooper, wanted to join them. However, the boys' mother, Olivia, did not think it was a good idea.

while he was traveling to road games. Other times, they were forced to listen to the home fans voicing their disappointment in another Saints loss.

Sometimes when Olivia would take Peyton and his brothers to watch their father play, some Saints fans booed Archie. The booing bothered Olivia, but her sons somehow knew they came with their father's job.

"During one game, the boos were upsetting Olivia until she turned around and saw Cooper and Peyton booing, too," Archie said. "They thought it went with the territory."[5]

Not everything was bad in New Orleans. Archie enjoyed good times with the Saints, too. He became the Saints' career passing leader in yards (21,734), completions (1,849), and attempts (3,335).

Archie's reputation around the NFL grew, too. He was voted the NFL's Most Valuable Player after passing for 3,416 yards and 17 touchdowns in 1978 and was voted to two Pro Bowls. Archie later played with the Houston Oilers in 1982–83 and the Minnesota Vikings in 1983–84.

When Archie was traded to the Oilers, he was forced to live in Houston while his family stayed in New Orleans. The boys missed their father for weeks at a time. Sometimes Archie would fly from Houston to New Orleans after practice, eat with the family, tuck the boys into bed, and fly back to Texas that

Archie and Peyton Manning leave Neyland Stadium in Knoxville, Tennessee, after a game in 1997.

night. Archie soon missed his kids too much to stay away. He retired from the NFL.

His new job as an analyst on Saints radio broadcasts allowed him to spend more time with his family while remaining a part of the game.

"Growing up in New Orleans as Archie Manning's son, I felt like a target. I've always known that whatever I do, people would hear about it. So I've had my guard up, and maybe that's molded my personality."

—Peyton Manning

Archie continues to be a popular figure in New Orleans, where he and Olivia still live.

While the teams around him did not finish high in the NFL standings, Archie still played his way into the hearts of NFL fans. His determination and dedication when times were tough made him an excellent role model for young Peyton and his brothers.

CHAPTER THREE

Brother in Arms

Even though Peyton Manning's father was an NFL quarterback, growing up with two brothers also helped drive Peyton to become the best football player he could be.

Peyton, the middle brother, is two years younger than Cooper and almost five years older than Eli.

While Archie Manning loved football, he did not want to force it on his sons. He encouraged his boys to try other sports and hobbies. But the Manning boys found sports all on their own, playing football, baseball, and basketball at early ages, just like their father.

Peyton began playing football not long after he could walk. He would play a scaled-down version of the game in the family living room at age three. From his knees, Archie would pass or hand off a miniature football to Peyton and Cooper or try to get past them

DID YOU KNOW?

Cooper Manning gave younger brother Peyton the nickname "Python."

on his way to an imaginary goal line. The Manning brothers could not get enough of the game indoors or outside.

As Peyton's hands grew, he began playing with a larger Nerf™ football, throwing passes to Cooper and Archie while trying not to break anything inside the house. They moved their games outside whenever possible. Eli eventually grew old enough to play alongside his brothers in the family football games, too.

Peyton and his brothers loved to suit up in kids' football equipment and pretend they were NFL stars like their father. They would wait for Archie to come home from practice and play quarterback for them and their neighborhood friends. While their famous father tried to teach the boys how to play the game correctly, he never made their games too serious. The Manning football games were designed to be fun, not work.

Peyton and big brother Cooper also got to play on a much larger field when they were young. Archie often brought his sons to work with him and let them play on the artificial turf of the massive Louisiana

Archie Manning throws a pass at Saints training camp in 1971.

Superdome. Before and after the Saints' practices and home games, the Manning boys could be found running, passing, catching, and tackling as if they were still in their front yard, rather than surrounded by more than 70,000 seats.

Cooper and Peyton learned their way around an NFL locker room when they were just preschoolers. The boys often roamed the team's locker room as if it were their own and talked to Saints players and coaches. Before games, the brothers even got the team's trainers to tape their ankles just like Archie's.

When the Manning boys grew bored with the Saints' locker room, they would find a ball and take it out to the Superdome field. When Archie was ready to begin pre-game stretching, he often found Cooper and Peyton wandering around the field talking to visiting NFL superstars without fear.

After the games, Archie let his sons hang out at his locker. While their father answered questions from the

DID YOU KNOW?

All three Manning brothers graduated from playing knee football with their father to the college ranks, winning scholarships to play football at Southeastern Conference schools. Cooper and Eli chose to attend the University of Mississippi. Peyton played at the University of Tennessee.

media, Cooper and Peyton picked up the tape that players took off their ankles, rolled it into a ball, and headed out to the Superdome field to play another game of "tape football."

Whether the Saints won or lost, the Manning boys enjoyed another day at their father's office. They did not understand how unusual Archie's job was.

"As much as we enjoyed going to them, Dad's games didn't dominate our lives. The next day, he'd be right back on the floor in the living room, playing 'knee' football," Cooper said.[1]

SIBLING RIVALRY

Archie and Olivia enjoyed watching their sons play together but came to realize that, as is the case with many brothers, the two oldest boys were becoming too competitive and playing rough with each other.

Peyton and Cooper still remember being very competitive growing up. They played their games hard. Peyton, as the younger brother, desperately wanted to prove that he was an equal to Cooper. Youngest brother Eli, who earned the nickname "Easy," didn't take part in his older brothers' squabbles.

Peyton was two years younger than Cooper, but he was about the same size, which made Peyton more aggressive toward his older brother. The Manning brothers' competitive natures often led them to join opposite teams and play so hard they'd begin to fight.

NFL quarterback brothers Eli (left) and Peyton Manning

Archie and Olivia grew more concerned when the boys regularly came home bloodied and crying. The boys' games no longer were just about having fun.

"I don't think there's ever been anyone more driven than Peyton," Cooper said. "He's always been wired. Whether it was football, or pickup basketball, he wanted to be the man in charge. That's his nature. Always has been."[2]

Archie now found himself forced to play the role of referee in their grudge matches. As Cooper and Peyton's father, it became his job to step between the boys and put an end to their outbursts. He tried to make them understand that brothers should enjoy each other rather than fight. At first, the boys did not want to listen.

"The day you two can finish a game without a fight will be a great day in my life," Archie once said. "You ought to be best friends. You don't know how lucky you are having a brother."[3]

Peyton also had to learn that his competitive nature could not give way to poor sportsmanship. After a youth basketball game, Peyton's coach told his players that they had lost due to a lack of

DID YOU KNOW?

Peyton did not play on an organized football team until he was thirteen. His father did not want him to play in local peewee leagues.

intensity. Peyton, age twelve, interrupted the coach. Peyton told him that he didn't know how to coach and that he had caused the team to lose the game. When Peyton told his father what had happened, Archie drove his son to the coach's house and demanded that Peyton apologize. Peyton told the coach he was sorry and learned a good lesson.

Peyton did not play organized football at a young age. Some of his friends played in peewee football leagues before they were teenagers. Archie did not think the leagues and coaches were organized to provide a good experience.

When Peyton entered seventh grade, Archie and Olivia finally let him play contact football for the first time. They hoped that Peyton could turn his competitive fire toward the opponents of the Isidore Newman School teams. But they soon discovered that nothing could keep Peyton and Cooper from pushing each other's brotherly competitive buttons, even when they were on the same team. Eventually, the Isidore Newman School helped the brothers begin playing together instead of against each other.

"From childhood, we were competitive to the extreme. We'd fight . . . he'd wrestle me down and let me know who was boss, and I'd get up and come back for more," Peyton said. "When we got older and realized the damage we could do, we confined our disagreements to arguing."[4]

Archie Manning talks about his sons Peyton (center) and Eli at a luncheon in New York April 22, 2004.

Archie began filming most of his sons' pickup games when they were young and continued his camera work as they grew up. When the brothers had settled down after the game, the family would enjoy watching the videos. These videos gave Peyton his first chance to watch himself perform. He would later learn to monitor his passing and footwork techniques by watching countless hours of video. The habit would stay with him through college and the pros.

Peyton proved to be more studious than Cooper in the classroom. While Cooper was a free spirit in school, Peyton studied hard to make good grades.

Today, Peyton no longer fights with his brothers. Peyton and Cooper are closer than ever. Even though Peyton plays for the Colts in Indianapolis, he keeps in close contact with Cooper in New Orleans. "Cooper is now my biggest fan, and I'm his," Peyton said. "He says, 'Peyton helps me get serious,' and I keep him loose. Life's a trade-off and that's ours."[5]

LITTLE BROTHER GROWS UP

Peyton isn't the only Manning brother to be selected with the very first pick of the NFL Draft. Five years after Peyton was selected by the Colts, younger brother Eli was acquired by the New York Giants after the San Diego Chargers drafted him first overall.

Eli's football career path has followed Peyton's in many ways, except one very important detour to college.

After quarterbacking Isidore Newman School to the state playoffs, Eli followed in his father's footsteps and played college football at the University of Mississippi.

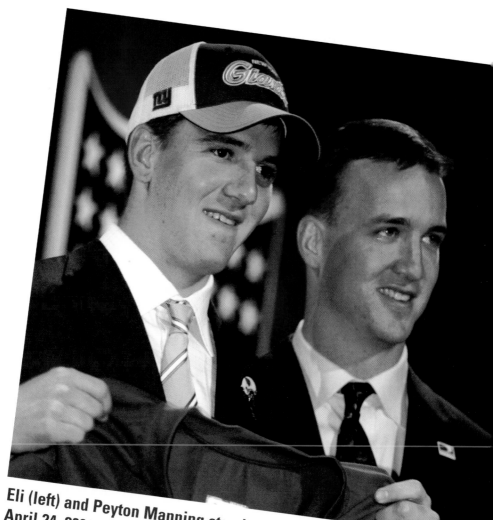

Eli (left) and Peyton Manning stand together at the NFL Draft April 24, 2004, in New York.

Like older brother Peyton, Eli elected to return to school for his senior season to enjoy one more year of college and to better prepare himself for a professional career.

While playing at Ole Miss, Eli broke many of his father's school records, including career touchdown passes and passing yards.

Archie helped Eli prepare for the NFL Draft. He remembered how playing for a poor team had made his pro career difficult. With that in mind, Archie and Eli asked the San Diego Chargers not to draft him with the first pick overall. The Mannings were not sure the Chargers would be the best team for Eli.

On the day of the 2004 NFL Draft, Eli, Archie, and even Peyton nervously waited to find out if the Chargers would draft Eli or whether they would let him slide down to another team. As the seconds ticked down on the Chargers' choice, NFL Commissioner Paul Tagliabue read the name on the team's draft card: Eli Manning.

While Eli and Archie spoke kindly of the Chargers, they still hoped he would start his NFL career with another team. Their wish came true a few picks later when the New York Giants selected North Carolina State quarterback Philip Rivers and then traded him to San Diego for the right to sign Eli to a pro contract.

The Giants wanted Eli to be their quarterback for many years to come.

After receiving news of the trade, Eli, Archie, and Peyton once again exited the NFL Draft with smiles on their faces.

CHAPTER FOUR

High School Hotshot

Playing high school football turned into an unforgettable experience, not only for Peyton Manning, but also for his family.

Peyton continued to play football because his older brother, Cooper, played.

"As sure as [Cooper] followed my dad into football, I followed him. At that point I'd probably have followed him anywhere," Peyton said. "And I'm not kidding when I say it. If he'd have opted for baseball out of high school, I might be trying to make a big league team right now instead of starring in the National Football League." [1]

After honing his skills from the seventh through ninth grades, Peyton was ready to be the man in charge.

"I don't ever want to play quarter-back again."

—Cooper Manning, after injuries forced him to fill in as Isidore Newman's quarterback during his sophomore season

"I'm glad now that Dad didn't let me play 'real' football until the seventh grade, because when I did, I was hungry," Peyton said. "I might not have loved it as much if I'd started earlier."[2]

In 1991, Peyton became the starting quarterback of his high school varsity football team. Though he was only a sophomore, Peyton was on the same level physically and mentally as the team's upperclassmen.

One day when Peyton and his father visited the Saints' practice facility, then-coach Jim Mora let the high school junior take some snaps with the professionals.

"The way he looks, the way he throws, I would have thought Peyton was a junior in college, not high school," Mora told Archie Manning.[3]

BROTHERS ON THE FIELD

Cooper was a senior receiver and team captain of a Newman High School team that usually lost more games than it won. Once Peyton arrived, the team took off like never before.

Football is extremely popular in Louisiana, but

Newman did not take football as seriously as many other New Orleans high schools. The Mannings sent their sons to the school because of its high academic standards rather than its athletic reputation. Not surprisingly, the Manning brothers set out to change the school's reputation in sports.

Cooper and Peyton urged their Newman football team to devote more time to improving. The brothers pushed their teammates to attend a new schedule of voluntary off-season workouts and to lift weights together.

Peyton organized passing drills in which he and his receivers, including Cooper, could practice their routes and timing. The extra focus on football paid off on the field. The Newman High School team showed a great deal of improvement with Cooper at receiver and Peyton gunning passes.

With Peyton and Cooper starring each week, every Newman game became a family affair for the Mannings. Before each home game, Archie and Olivia Manning would arrive early and set up a tailgate party in the stadium parking lot before joining friends in the stands. Archie would bring his video camera and enjoy watching his sons play. He knew that Peyton would want to study his own performance after the game.

Peyton's father took care to avoid coaching his sons from the stands. He just wanted to enjoy the results of their hard work. Today, Peyton fondly remembers those high school games.

"Dad was my role model, the place to go for knowledge about the game. I couldn't have had a better example to follow on, or off the field," Peyton said. "Cooper was my goad, and though he was a pain in the butt a lot of time, he is now my best friend. Could anyone have had it any better?"[4]

No one played better than the Manning boys. In their only season together on the Newman varsity squad, Peyton and Cooper teamed up to set several school records. They combined for 73 completions, 1,250 yards, and 13 touchdowns. The two brothers who once fought each time they played were now a team that couldn't be stopped.

Peyton still remembers how much fun he had passing to his brother.

"For a quarterback, there's nothing like having your brother as your primary receiver," Peyton said. "You're on the same genetic wavelength. You know each other's every move. And you've been living in the same house together all your lives. How could you beat that?"[5]

Hard work and dedication may have helped the Newman team, but there was another secret to the Manning boys' uncanny chemistry. Peyton and Cooper borrowed hand signals from their sandlot days to help communicate pass patterns.

Peyton and Archie Manning watch campers at the Manning
Passing Academy.

"Unbeknownst to the coaches, Cooper and I worked out our own set of signals for that season. We didn't tell anybody but Dad," Peyton said. "If I touched my nose, it was a comeback pass. Tap my helmet and it was a curl. It wasn't exactly fair to the other receivers, but it was working and we were winning."[6]

The Manning boys led Newman to a 9–1 season and a rare trip to the state playoffs that year. In the second round of the playoffs, Port Barre tried to stop the dynamic duo by double-teaming Cooper. The coverage tactic worked for a few series, but leave it to the Manning boys to find a solution.

With the game tied at 14, the coach told Cooper to run a 10-yard hook pattern, but Peyton had other ideas. He told his brother to go deep if the defensive back played bump-and-run. Cooper zoomed past the defender and caught a 60-yard touchdown pass that put Newman ahead for good.

Newman's miracle season later came to an end in the state semifinal game against Haynesville High. The game's outcome wasn't decided until the last two minutes. Trailing 27–21, Newman was driving toward a possible game-winning touchdown until Peyton threw an interception with thirty seconds left in the game.

Peyton was devastated by the loss, but his family was there to support him. Cooper wrapped his arm around his younger brother to console him and let him know everything would be all right.

While the disappointing loss was Cooper's final game at Newman High School, his legacy lived on there. The Manning brothers helped lead the school to new heights as a football power in New Orleans.

The next season, Peyton would throw 30 touchdown passes and lead Newman to the state quarterfinals. When Peyton was a senior, Newman's coach opened up the offense and let Peyton throw the ball early and often. That year, Peyton completed 168 of 265 passes for 2,703 yards and 39 touchdowns. Newman finished the regular season undefeated.

Tennessee quarterback Peyton Manning looks for a receiver.

In the second round of the playoffs, Newman

45

faced the North East High team from Zachary, which was coached by former NFL quarterback and Super Bowl Most Valuable Player Doug Williams. Both teams' offenses were hitting on all cylinders. Peyton had an exceptional day. He completed 23 of 42 passes for 395 yards and 3 touchdowns. But North East's offense put up even bigger numbers and outlasted Newman, 39–28.

Newman's quest for a state title was denied, but Peyton's high school legacy was set. With Peyton at quarterback, Newman won 34 games and lost only 5 during his three varsity seasons.

After the season, he was named to several All-American teams and was voted Most Valuable Player in Louisiana for his classification. He also was selected as the nation's top high school offensive player by the Touchdown Club of Columbus, Ohio—the same organization that had twice named his father college player of the year.

Peyton and his parents were especially proud of his making the Blue Chip Academic All-America squad, an honor for academic and athletic achievements. The award proved that Peyton could devote time to academics and athletics successfully.

CRISIS FOR COOPER

When Cooper accepted a scholarship to play football at his father's alma mater Ole Miss, fans across the

South thought Peyton would follow his older brother two years later.

And they were right. Famous coaches from powerful college football programs were sending letters with hopes that Peyton would come play quarterback for their teams, but he wanted to play pass-and-catch with his older brother again. Peyton was determined to play quarterback at Ole Miss as soon as possible.

Those dreams faded when Cooper noticed numbness in his right hand and leg. When the symptoms recurred, doctors diagnosed Cooper with spinal stenosis, or a narrowing of the spinal column in his neck.

The condition would not keep Cooper from living a normal life, but if he continued to play football, he would risk being paralyzed. Cooper would never play football again. The Manning family was devastated.

Peyton had to play in a baseball game the day that Cooper underwent surgery to correct his condition. After the game, his coach told Peyton to go straight to the hospital. Something was wrong. He found his family in the hospital chapel praying for Cooper.

DID YOU KNOW?

Peyton also lettered in baseball and basketball at Isidore Newman School. He was named second-team All-State shortstop his senior season.

Hours after the surgery, doctors had found a blood clot. Cooper needed more surgery to prevent paralysis. Fortunately, the second surgery was successful. Cooper would recover but without football in his future.

Doctors later examined Peyton. He did not suffer from a similar condition. Peyton would be okay, but he would have to go on playing football without his big brother. It would take some time to get used to the idea of never throwing another pass to Cooper.

When college coaches and scouts were allowed to contact Peyton, he received as many as thirty telephone calls a day. Each hoped to lure Peyton to his school.

Now that Cooper no longer was playing at Ole Miss, Peyton allowed himself to consider playing for other big-time colleges. He wanted to experience other schools, so he made unofficial visits to universities such as Florida, Florida State, Texas, and Texas A&M.

These trips made Ole Miss fans very nervous. They asked Archie Manning how any son of his could think about playing for a school other than his alma mater. Archie always told them that he wanted Peyton to go to Ole Miss but that he told his son to pick whichever college he wanted to attend.

Coaches from prestigious football schools such as Michigan and Notre Dame joined the recruiting chase, stopping by the Manning home to chat with Peyton and his parents. Peyton weighed each school's coach and football program in his mind as the signing deadline neared. His final decision came down to two schools: Ole Miss and Tennessee.

Hordes of fans anxiously awaited his announcement. Peyton chose to play football for Tennessee. Though he had grown up rooting for his father's alma mater, Peyton didn't want the special treatment that could have come with his playing at Ole Miss. He also realized that the larger, more

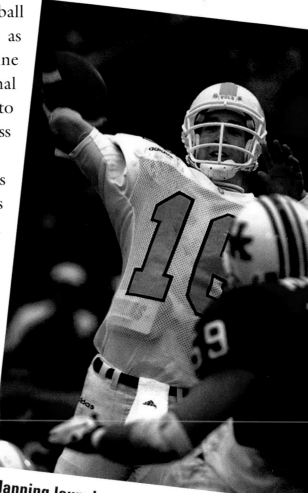

Manning launches a pass during a win against Kentucky in 1997.

successful program and passing offense at Tennessee was more suited to transforming him into the best quarterback he could be.

CHAPTER FIVE

5
Tennessee Volunteer

Playing at Tennessee introduced Manning to one of college football's greatest game day experiences, as well as all the pressures and expectations that go along with it.

More than 100,000 Volunteer fans converge on Tennessee's Neyland Stadium for each home game. Many even float down the Tennessee River and dock their boats alongside the massive stadium. It seems as if the entire city of Knoxville turns into a sea of orange and white.

All of those Tennessee fans were ready to focus their emotions on their prized freshman quarterback, Peyton Manning.

As Manning prepared to make the transition from high school to college, he knew that he could not rest on his Newman High laurels. He arrived on campus early, determined to work with Tennessee's upperclassmen and coaches as often as possible before the season started. He had his sights set on doing whatever he could to help the Volunteers win a Southeastern Conference championship.

Tennessee's quarterback depth chart included senior starter Jerry Colquitt and junior backup Todd Helton. They were followed by Manning and freshman Branndon Stewart, who were competing for third- and fourth-string. Freshmen quarterbacks, even highly regarded recruits such as Manning and Stewart, rarely see much playing time. Manning didn't think he would play much as a freshman, but he prepared as if he were the team's starter.

"I was hoping to play some as a freshman; Coach Fulmer had said I might," Manning said. "I made up my mind to go in with the best possible attitude and best possible work ethic." [1]

Manning's foresight, attitude, and preparation paid off in the Volunteers' season-opening game against UCLA.

> "I made up my mind to go in with the best possible attitude and best possible work ethic."
>
> **—Peyton Manning**

He watched as Colquitt was sidelined by an injury in the game's opening minutes. When Helton proved unable to move the Volunteer offense, Tennessee coach Phillip Fulmer called Manning's number. Manning couldn't believe that he was going to play in his first college game.

But he never got to throw a pass. He handed the ball off on three consecutive running plays before the Volunteers punted. Manning went back to the bench. He was disappointed but even more determined to stay prepared for his next opportunity to play.

Three games later, Helton injured his knee against Mississippi State. Manning was called again, and this time he would be asked to pass. He made the best of his opportunity, throwing a 76-yard touchdown pass in a narrow 3-point loss. Tennessee fans began chanting for their outstanding freshman to get the next start.

The following week, Coach Fulmer named Manning his starting quarterback. The debut would not be an easy one. The next team on the Volunteers' schedule was nationally-ranked Washington State, which had not allowed a touchdown in their three wins.

Before the game, Fulmer explained that he wanted Manning to play conservatively. He wanted his inexperienced quarterback to be careful passing the ball and to avoid interceptions. Manning thought he was ready to run the entire Tennessee offensive playbook, but he understood. Fulmer wanted to put

Manning runs toward the end zone to score a touchdown in a September 9, 1995, game against Georgia.

Manning in a position to succeed. He wanted to give his young quarterback a chance to get his feet under him before asking him to carry the team.

In his first game as a starter, Manning only threw 14 passes, but he completed half of them for a total of 79 yards. The most memorable of those completions was his longest pass, a 41-yard bomb that put the Volunteers deep in Washington State territory and led to the winning score. Fulmer was especially proud that Manning did not commit a turnover—a fumble or an interception—in his first game.

Fulmer's faith in his freshman quarterback "meant a lot to me, " Manning said. [2]

Entrenched as the Volunteers' starting quarterback, he grew more confident with each game. He completed more than 60 percent of his pass attempts and threw just 6 interceptions. He was even more proud that he helped contribute to seven wins in his eight games as a starter.

In a little more than half a season as Tennessee's starting quarterback, Manning passed for 1,141 yards and 11 touchdowns, good enough to be named Southeastern Conference Freshman of the Year.

He even played well in his first postseason bowl game. Against Virginia Tech in the Gator Bowl, he completed 12 of 19 passes for 189 yards and even scrambled—as his father used to—for 29 yards.

Manning's determination had suited him well in his freshman season, but he wanted to continue to improve the following season. He knew the only way to accomplish that goal was to work hard on and off the field.

Even though Manning allowed some time for his girlfriend, Ashley, he spent most of his time in the classroom, practice field, or in his room studying the Volunteers' playbook. During the summer, he also attended classes toward his degree.

When reporters called the Tennessee football office late at night to interview coaches, Manning often

Manning looks downfield in a game against Texas Tech.

answered the phone. He was there studying game videos. His friends called him "Caveman" and his room "The Cave" because he spent so much time in the dark watching game videos of upcoming opponents.

The Tennessee coaching staff was impressed with Manning's study habits. They had never seen a college football player spend so much time learning the ins and outs of his team and his opponents. "He was like a sponge for information," Fulmer said.[3]

COACH AND MENTOR

Neither the nicknames nor the long hours bothered Manning. He wasn't in college to have fun. He was there to learn.

"If I wasn't in class, I was doing something to make myself a better football player," he said.[4]

Manning's study habits and grasp of the Volunteers' offensive schemes had a positive effect on the coach directly charged with his performance. Tennessee's offensive coordinator, David Cutcliffe, had to study harder with Manning around. The young quarterback asked questions that Cutcliffe and veteran Tennessee quarterbacks couldn't answer right away.

While spending so much time together, Manning and Cutcliffe developed a close relationship on and off the field.

"We developed something all quarterbacks and offensive coordinators need to have—total

Manning calls signals during his team's win against Arkansas November 16, 1996, in Knoxville, Tennessee.

communication, available around the clock," Manning said. "With Coach Cut, I had a mix of coach and friend. We didn't just talk about football. We talked about life."[5]

Manning's hard work with Cutcliffe paid off as Tennessee won nine regular-season games during his sophomore season. The team's only loss was an embarrassing rout by arch-rival Florida.

Manning's accuracy was better than ever. He completed 244 of 380 passes for 2,954 yards and 22 touchdowns, while throwing an NCAA record low 4 interceptions. Better yet, Tennessee's victory against Ohio State in the Citrus Bowl left the Volunteers ranked third in the country at year's end.

Never satisfied, Manning continued to hone his skills and mastery of the Volunteer offense.

In Manning's junior season, the Volunteers once again faced off against Florida in a crucial Southeastern Conference contest. Things looked bleak as the Gators jumped out to an early 35–0 lead, but Manning remained determined to bring his team back. Although Manning completed a school-record 37 passes in 65 tries for 492 yards, the Volunteers came up short in the end, 35–29.

The Volunteers finished the season with a somewhat disappointing 10–2 record, but Manning further etched his name into Tennessee football history as the school's first quarterback to pass for more than 3,000 yards.

As the clock wound down on Tennessee's 39–27 win against Northwestern in the Citrus Bowl, Volunteer fans chanted, "One more year! One more year!"[6] They were hoping that they weren't watching Manning's last game in orange and white. After his junior season, he was eligible to make himself available for the NFL Draft.

STAY OR MOVE ON?

After the Volunteers finished the year ranked second in the nation, there was no doubt that Manning was the king of Tennessee. The city of Knoxville named a street Peyton Manning Pass, and the zoo named a baby giraffe after the star quarterback. While Manning loved playing in Knoxville, he still faced a tough decision. Should he return to Tennessee for his senior season or leave early for the NFL?

Manning had already earned enough classroom credits to graduate from Tennessee with a degree in speech communication. He was considered not only the next year's leading Heisman Trophy candidate but also the NFL's top draft pick.

Manning's options made for a tough decision. He

DID YOU KNOW?

Earning a college education and diploma was important to Manning. While many college players take the minimum number of classes, Manning balanced a heavy class load with football practice and games at Tennessee. He earned enough class credits to graduate by the end of his junior year.

likely could make several million dollars as a rookie NFL quarterback, but he also wanted to come back to Tennessee for another shot at a national championship. In addition, he would enter the season as a favorite to win the Heisman Trophy. But what would happen to his pro prospects if he were injured during his senior season?

After seeking the advice of his family, Manning talked to NFL quarterbacks and other athletes who had faced the same dilemma, including Troy Aikman, Drew Bledsoe, and Michael Jordan.

In March 1997, the sports world anxiously waited as Manning stepped to the microphone at a press conference to announce his decision. Tennessee fans cheered: He would play one more year for the Volunteers.

"I looked at the money," Manning said. "But remaining a college student was strongest in my heart." [7]

Having made that life-changing decision, Manning set out to lead the Volunteers to a national championship. While he proved to be the nation's top quarterback, he fell just short of realizing his dream of a national title.

In a record-breaking performance against Kentucky, he passed for 523 yards, but the feat came after a fourth consecutive loss to Florida that cost the Volunteers a shot at a national championship.

Manning finished with 36 touchdowns and 3,819 yards. He led Tennessee to an SEC championship and

TENNESSEE TITAN

In his four years at the University of Tennessee, Peyton Manning set 42 NCAA, SEC, and school career and single-game records. Here are just a few:

CAREER RECORDS

Passing yards	11,201
Passing touchdowns	89
Pass attempts	1,381
Pass completions	863
Winning percentage	.867
Wins as starting QB	39

SINGLE-GAME RECORDS

Passing yards	523
Pass attempts	65
Pass completions	37

"College is supposed to be the best four years of your life.... These are the times that will stay with me."

—Peyton Manning

the Orange Bowl to cap off his final collegiate season. Those numbers earned him many honors, including the Sullivan Award, which is given to the nation's top amateur athlete. He also was named to many All-America teams. He later became the first Tennessee player to have his jersey retired.

But another college football honor eluded Manning, just as it had his father. Manning finished second to Michigan's Charles Woodson in voting for the Heisman Trophy.

Even though Manning's senior year did not include a national championship or Heisman Trophy, he did not regret his decision to play four years at Tennessee.

"College is supposed to be the best four years of your life. I made a lot of friends in college. I created a bunch of memories. These are the times that will stay with me," he said. "You can talk about the awards, but that isn't what's important."[8]

CHAPTER SIX

NFL Franchise Rookie

After Peyton Manning entered his name in the 1998 NFL Draft, the only suspense was whether he would be the first or second player selected. Washington State quarterback Ryan Leaf was also highly rated.

For several months prior to the draft, sports reporters and talk-radio hosts debated which of the prized picks would make the best NFL quarterback.

Some critics thought Leaf's arm was stronger than Manning's. Others said Manning's ability to study playbooks and defenses gave him an advantage. Both quarterbacks possessed winning collegiate resumes, but some critics looked at Manning's four losses against Florida and questioned his ability to win big games.

Manning smiles after being picked first in the NFL Draft.

Both Manning and Leaf used private workouts with the representatives of NFL teams to make their best cases for being the first pick of the draft.

After the workout, Colts owner Robert Irsay sent his private jet to fly Manning to Florida, where the two spent some time getting to know each other.

"I think he liked me. I know I liked him," Manning said. "So as I was leaving, I said, 'You know, Mr. Irsay, I'll win for you.'"[1]

The confident statement from the young quarterback from Tennessee impressed the Colts' owner. Irsay later said that he remembered those words when it came time for the Colts to make their draft choice.

When the Indianapolis Colts handed their choice to NFL commissioner Paul Tagliabue, the decision between Manning and Leaf became clear: The Colts wanted to build the future of their franchise around Manning.

In the minds of Irsay and Colts general manager Bill Polian, Manning's maturity and poise raised him above the competition. They believed that the work ethic and determination he had exhibited at Tennessee would help him evolve into one of the NFL's best quarterbacks and help their team drive to a future Super Bowl.

"Peyton is a franchise quarterback," Irsay said.[2]

At the draft in New York City, Manning had his

"Peyton is so much farther along than I was when I came into the league. He's ready for this challenge."

—Archie Manning

picture taken holding a number 18 Colts jersey, and then asked his father to join him on the stage. Considering Archie had been the second pick of the 1971 NFL Draft, the son was following in his proud father's footsteps again.

Before Manning could put on a Colts uniform in a game, he and his agents had to negotiate his rookie contract with the team. As the top pick, Manning was expected to receive millions of dollars over several years, but it took a while for his agents and the Colts to agree on the amount.

Manning was not happy as the negotiations dragged on and on, but he knew that his first NFL contract was an important one. His rookie contract would establish a base for the rest of his NFL career.

"I was hoping my contract negotiations would go smoothly. I didn't want them to be confrontational, and I knew I didn't want to be one of those 'shameful holdouts,'" Manning said. "I wound up being a holdout myself."[3]

Manning's "holdout" lasted only four days. As soon as his agents and the Colts agreed to a contract,

Peyton and Archie Manning arrive at the Colts' headquarters.

DID YOU KNOW?

Peyton Manning agreed to a rookie contract that paid him $48 million over six seasons with the Colts. He also was paid millions of dollars to endorse credit cards, phones, shoes, and electronics. When Manning discovered that he was going to be paid so much money to play a game he loved, he started the PeyBack Foundation, a charitable group designed to aid youth programs.

he was on the practice field trying to make up for the sessions he had missed.

NEW KID ON THE TEAM

An NFL training camp can be overwhelming for a rookie quarterback. Manning spent the summer months learning the team's playbook and players. He threw pass after pass in drills and scrimmages prior to the Colts' first preseason game, which would be Manning's first appearance in a Colts uniform.

Once Manning was in the Colts' lineup, it didn't take him long to prove the Colts had made the right decision. Manning's first NFL pass was a 48-yard touchdown to Marvin Harrison in the preseason opener against the Seattle Seahawks. Like all rookie quarterbacks, Manning's learning curve included good times and bad. He struggled to adjust to the unforgiving speed of NFL defenders and bristled any time he made a mistake. Manning was determined to learn from his errors.

After Manning learned the Colts' offensive play-book during training camp, Indianapolis made a surprising decision. The team's general manager and coach decided to make Manning the starting quarterback for his first NFL regular-season game.

Many NFL teams like to protect their rookie quarterbacks by letting them learn the game from the sidelines. Now, at the age of twenty-two, Manning was going to be the seventh youngest NFL player to start at quarterback.

"We're putting him in there right away," Coach Jim Mora said. "We didn't draft this guy number one to sit on the bench."[4]

Just as in college, Manning's study habits helped him prepare for the start of the regular season. His first real test was against the Miami Dolphins' defense in week one. On his first play, Manning read the Dolphins' blitz and dumped the ball off to

DID YOU KNOW?
When Peyton Manning signed his lucrative rookie contract, his Colts teammates gave the quarterback the nickname "Powerball" after the lottery game.

> ## "We didn't draft this guy number one to sit on the bench."
>
> ### —Jim Mora

running back Marshall Faulk for a big gain.

Manning made running the Colts' offense look easy. He completed his first three passes before a Colts running back fumbled to the Dolphins.

On his next possession, Manning learned a tough NFL lesson. When he threw the ball to an open Marvin Harrison, a Miami defensive back stepped in front of the receiver. He made the interception and returned it for a touchdown.

By the end of the game, Manning had thrown 3 interceptions but also passed for a touchdown and more than 300 yards in the loss to the Dolphins.

After the game, legendary Dolphins quarterback Dan Marino looked for Manning as the teams shook hands at midfield. Marino, the NFL's all-time leading passer, wanted to congratulate the rookie on his impressive debut.

While Manning was disappointed with the loss and less than satisfied with his performance, he didn't give up or get down. And Mora didn't take him out of the lineup. No matter how many mistakes Manning made early in his first NFL season, the Colts stuck by their number one pick through four straight losses to open the season.

"Coach, I really appreciate your hanging with me this year," Manning would later tell Mora.[5] His coach told him, "You can't learn from the sidelines, Peyton."[6]

Manning responded to the Colts' patience with steady improvement, especially in the fourth quarters of games. Once he had spent a few quarters figuring out opposing defenses, he was better able to find their weaknesses and make them pay late in the game.

In week five, Manning and the Colts took the field against the San Diego Chargers, the team that had drafted Ryan Leaf. The chance to compare the two rookie quarterbacks at the center of that year's draft drew the attention of many NFL fans and reporters.

Some wondered if the Colts had made a mistake drafting Manning. Leaf and the Chargers had already won two games, while Manning and the Colts were looking for their first win of the season.

Manning knew that quarterbacks don't play against each other; they play against opposing teams' defenses. So, he tried to downplay the pre-game hype. The game would be two NFL teams playing against each other, not two rookie quarterbacks.

While neither Manning nor Leaf played very well, the Colts did manage to win their first game of the season. With his first NFL victory under his belt, Manning, his teammates, and their coaches were relieved. Yet they remained determined to keep improving.

WORKING HARD, GETTING BETTER

Manning and the Colts' offense showed steady improvement as the season wore on, but the Indianapolis defense struggled to hold on to leads. As a result, the Colts lost many frustrating games in the fourth quarter.

At the end of a long season, the Colts' record was 3–13. Even though the team's finish was as expected, Manning's performance reinforced the Colts' decision to draft him number one. He set NFL rookie records with 326 completions in 575 attempts, 3,739 passing yards, and 26 touchdowns. He was also named to the NFL All-Rookie team.

The Colts' coaches were happy their young quarterback had shown great improvement reading defenses, executing plays, and leading the offense. They had no doubts about the future of their number one pick.

Manning was proud that he was the only NFL quarterback to play every down that season. Despite having

DID YOU KNOW?

Manning asked the Colts to assign him a locker among the team's offensive linemen. He wanted to be one of the guys and get to know the players assigned to protect him.

huge defenders chase him around the pocket and enduring many sacks, he took all 982 snaps from center and proved that he was a durable quarterback at the professional level.

"I learned a lot in every single one of [my rookie] games, whether it was a third quarter of a blowout or a two-minute drill where we had a chance to win," he said. "The best thing I did was to show the guys I'm here to work." [7]

As he packed up his locker after the season, Manning didn't sulk or brood. He was already thinking of ways to improve his play and lead the Colts to more victories in his second season.

"It was frustrating and disappointing," he said. "But you can either sit there and feel sorry for yourself or learn from it and do something about it." [8]

After the season, Manning asked his father to fly to Indianapolis and help him prepare to move back to New Orleans for the off-season. Manning had not spent much time with his father during the long NFL season. He wanted to use the long thirteen-hour drive to New Orleans for some quality one-on-one time with his father.

CHAPTER SEVEN

Breakthrough Season

After a trying but encouraging rookie season, Manning was determined to make the Colts a better team in 1999. So he made a list of all the things he wanted to accomplish in that season. Manning began setting goals as a guide.

"An athlete has to have goals—for a day, for a lifetime," Manning said, "and I like to put mine in writing so that afterward I can check the design against the finished product."[1]

Manning wanted to see himself and the team improve in every aspect of their performances. Little did he know that his second professional season would produce results beyond even his lofty expectations.

As a quarterback in high school and college,

Manning always tried to lead by example. He expected his teammates to practice and play hard, too. After spending his rookie season learning the NFL game and getting to know his Colts teammates, he was ready to become an even stronger leader as a pro quarterback. He made it his job to continue to earn respect from his teammates.

"Last year we hoped we could win games. This year we really do believe we can win and that helps you play better."

–Peyton Manning prior to the Colts' 1999 breakthrough season

"My rookie year I didn't take control as much," he said. "I was a bit more reserved. You want to earn the respect of your teammates before you start barking orders."[2]

The Colts were active in the off-season. They traded Marshall Faulk to St. Louis, and then used the draft pick they got to select running back Edgerrin James from the University of Miami. The Colts also added players to strengthen their defense. The moves left Manning and Colts fans excited about the upcoming season. But there was still much work to do.

Manning and his receivers practiced together

Manning is chased by the Chiefs'
Reggie Tongue in a 1999 game.

often during the off-season and spent a lot of time together off the field with the hope of developing better chemistry on the field.

Running pass routes over and over helped Manning and his receivers develop better timing and knowledge of the decisions each would make during a game. A close bond between a quarterback and his receivers can mean the difference between an incompletion and a touchdown pass.

Manning also spent extra time improving his passing techniques. Even though he had produced outstanding passing statistics, he knew that he could always be better.

Manning knew even professional quarterbacks must work on the details of their throwing motions. He tried to improve his footwork and setup in the pocket. He concentrated on basic passing fundamentals, such as how the ball came off his hand.

With his first NFL season under his belt and a second round of mini-camps and training camp, Manning had a better grasp of the Colts' playbook. He picked up on opposing defenses more quickly and more readily recognized where to direct the ball. He had a better feeling for which play would work or if he should change the play—or audible—at the line of scrimmage.

A second NFL training camp also made him more confident in his abilities as a professional quarterback.

Manning's emergence as the Colts' team leader

during the off-season paid off when the 1999 season began. Before the first game against the Buffalo Bills, Manning pulled the offense aside and challenged his teammates to succeed.

"We're not going 3–13 this year. We're better. We've worked hard. Let's stay together, be positive, get a fast start and have a killer instinct," Manning said. [3]

The inspirational speech worked. The Colts opened the season with a 31–14 victory against the Bills. In the game, Manning was very accurate, completing 21 of 33 passes for 284 yards and 2 touchdowns. The Colts' defense also showed improvement, limiting the Bills to a touchdown and 2 field goals.

Unfortunately, the Colts' positive start took a detour in the following weeks. They blew a big lead at New England, beat San Diego, and then lost a thriller at Miami in which Manning threw 2 touchdown passes. After four games, the Colts found themselves at 2–2 but feeling as if they were better than a .500 team.

They were right.

THE START OF SOMETHING BIG

The team was about to shock the NFL world. Their fifth game of the season, which was against the Jets, would be the start of something big. The 16–13 win against their AFC East rivals was the first in an unthinkable streak of eleven consecutive victories.

The Colts' offensive power was something to behold. Manning and Harrison, in just their second season together, had established themselves as one of the NFL's best pass-catch combinations. The Colts' passing game was complemented by the running of James, who was on his way to being named AFC Rookie of the Year. Even the Colts' kicking game was greatly improved with Mike Vanderjagt converting 34 of 38 field-goal attempts.

Best of all, the Colts' offensive line protected their second-year quarterback. Manning was sacked just fifteen times in sixteen games. He no longer had to drop back in the pocket expecting to be hurried or sacked.

As the Colts added win after win during their surprising streak, they found themselves rising up the NFL standings and within reach of the unthinkable. They clinched a playoff berth in week fourteen and won the AFC East the week after that.

The Colts' long winning streak ended on the last week of the season with a loss in the cold of Buffalo, but the Colts' 13–3 record—following a 3–13 finish

Manning talks with wide receiver Marvin Harrison on the sidelines during a 2005 preseason game against Buffalo.

in 1998—amounted to the biggest one-year turnaround in NFL history. Manning and the Colts had ascended from the NFL's basement to the AFC East's penthouse.

Before the playoffs began, Manning, James, and Harrison—who came to be known as "The Triplets"—were voted to their first Pro Bowl. Manning had put together an outstanding year. He completed 62 percent of his passes while setting a new Colts' record with 4,135 passing yards. He also threw 13 fewer interceptions than during his rookie season and produced 26 touchdown passes.

Manning, James, and Harrison also gave the Colts a statistical rarity: 4,000 passing yards, 1,000 rushing yards, and 1,000 receiving yards. Few NFL teams had ever enjoyed having the conference leaders in passing, rushing, and receiving all performing on the field at the same time.

POSTSEASON DEBUT

However, the Pro Bowl in Hawaii would have to wait. Manning, James, and Harrison were about to host the franchise's first postseason game in Indianapolis. The Colts drew another team that had surprised the NFL with its success. The Tennessee Titans finished second in the AFC Central with a 13–3 record. The Titans would be playing in only their third playoff game since 1993.

The Titans were coming off an exciting wild-card win against Buffalo. In that game, Kevin Dyson had received a desperation lateral from Frank Wychek on a kickoff to score the last-second, game-winning touchdown that came to be known as the "Music City Miracle."

Before a sold-out crowd in the RCA Dome, the Colts took an early lead against the Titans on two field goals by Vanderjagt. The Colts led 9–6 at halftime.

The Titans' defense kept Manning, James, and Harrison in check, holding the Colts' offense well below its usual output. Running back Eddie George rushed for a team playoff-record 162 yards, including a 68-yard touchdown that gave the Titans the lead for good.

The Colts' attempts to rally in the fourth quarter were particularly tough on Manning. He completed just 4 of 16 passes for 42 yards in the final quarter. His 15-yard run was too little, too late in the 19–16 loss.

The Titans' defense, headed by AFC sack leader Jevon Kearse, put pressure on Manning much of the day. Manning's statistics reflected that he had to rush his decisions and passes. He completed just 19 of 42 passes for 227 yards and no touchdowns.

Tennessee would go on to win the AFC Championship game and play in Super Bowl XXXIV. The Titans fell one yard short in a loss to the St. Louis Rams in the Super Bowl.

While Manning was disappointed with the early postseason exit, he did not dwell on the loss. He looked ahead to making his third NFL season even more successful.

"You can't just talk about how well things went last year," Manning said. "That's over with. This is all about today. We're going to set our expectations pretty high."[4]

COLTS' BREAKTHROUGH SEASON
1999

REGULAR SEASON

Week 1	W 31-14	Buffalo
Week 2	L 28–31	at New England
Week 3	W 27–19	at San Diego
Week 4	Bye	
Week 5	L 31–34	Miami
Week 6	W 16–13	at New York Jets
Week 7	W 31–10	Cincinnati
Week 8	W 34–24	Dallas
Week 9	W 25–17	Kansas City
Week 10	W 27–19	at New York Giants
Week 11	W 44–17	at Philadelphia
Week 12	W 13–6	New York Jets
Week 13	W 37–34	at Miami
Week 14	W 20–15	New England
Week 15	W 24–21	Washington
Week 16	W 29–28	at Cleveland
Week 17	L 6–31	at Buffalo

POST SEASON

Divisional Playoff	L 16–19	Tennessee

CHAPTER EIGHT

Manning and Harrison

Through the years, Manning found his favorite target again and again—receiver Marvin Harrison. On October 17, 2005, in a game against St. Louis, Manning and Harrison made NFL history. Manning's 6-yard pass to Harrison was the 86th touchdown pass between the two, making them the NFL's most prolific touchdown duo.

The record-setting play showed how the quarterback and receiver had become such a successful combination. They always play in sync with each other. Manning took a short drop before lofting the ball toward the back corner of the end zone. Harrison faked the St. Louis defender off the line of scrimmage and then faded to the back of the end

After catching a touchdown pass, Harrison walks off with Manning.

zone. When the ball dropped over Harrison's shoulder, he quickly dragged both feet inbounds to complete the pass.

The historic pass lifted Manning and Harrison past NFL Hall of Famers Steve Young and Jerry Rice, who combined for 85 touchdowns with the San Francisco 49ers.

After the record-breaking touchdown, Manning ran to speak to his favorite receiver. Was there a problem? The dynamic duo could not decide which player would keep the football used on the record-breaking play. No, it wasn't a case of selfishness. In fact, it was the opposite. It turns out Manning wanted Harrison to keep the ball, and Harrison wanted Manning to take it. The moment between the quarterback and receiver became as special as their teamwork on the field.

DID YOU KNOW?
Peyton Manning and Marvin Harrison combined for 3 touchdowns in a game against New Orleans September 28, 2003.

"I just kind of went over there to congratulate him and he kind of gave me the ball and I sort of gave it back to him," Manning later said. "He gave it to me and I said, 'No,' so we decided we're going to split it somehow."[1]

Having set so

many NFL records together, you would think that Manning and Harrison would be used to such decisions. They have combined for more pass completions and yards than any other quarterback-receiver duo in the history of the NFL.

SHARED SUCCESS

Manning and Harrison would make more history in their eighth season together. One month later, they became the first NFL quarterback–wide receiver duo to combine for more than 10,000 career yards. They also have shared more completions than any other passing tandem.

"Having those records would mean a lot—that two guys can do what we've done in such a short time," Manning said after just eight years of playing with Harrison. "It's a product of the work we've done together."[2]

When Manning began his rookie season with the Colts, he could not have asked for a better receiver than Harrison, who was the team's first pick

DID YOU KNOW?

Marvin Harrison was a star football and basketball player at Roman Catholic High School in Philadelphia. He played football at Syracuse University in New York, where he caught passes from quarterback Donovan McNabb, who went on to the Philadelphia Eagles.

Harrison talks with Manning after the Colts defeated the Cleveland Browns December 15, 2002.

(nineteenth overall) of the 1996 NFL Draft and came from Syracuse. Besides blazing speed, lightning-quick feet, and sticky hands, Harrison also had the desire and dedication to make the Colts' offense the best it could be.

But the quarterback and receiver still needed time to get on the same page of the Colts' playbook. There were pass routes and defensive reads to get down pat, as well as timing and instinct. It would take many practices and hours of game experience before they were thinking as one.

"We went through bumps and bruises that first year or two," Harrison said. "But we've developed a rapport where we can do things without speaking."[3]

Harrison is the most productive receiver in the Colts' distinguished history. He holds team records for receptions, receiving touchdowns, and total yards from scrimmage. He set the NFL record for receptions in a season with 143 in 2002. He is the only NFL player with 100-plus receptions in four straight seasons (1999–2002). He also is the only NFL player to post back-to-back 1,500-yard seasons.

Not long after they broke the Young-Rice touchdown record, another pass from Manning pushed Harrison over the 12,000-yard mark for his career. It was a case of one perfectionist teaming up with another.

"Harrison is such a technician, a craftsman," Colts coach Tony Dungy said. "He's not satisfied with just catching a ball or making a big play. He wants to be perfect on everything, and he works that way. If he drops a certain kind of ball, a certain catch, he'll make that catch 25 to 30 times in practice."[4]

Perhaps it's true that practice makes perfect.

Manning once estimated that he throws 33 passes to Harrison in a typical practice. And they put in extra work after practice, running what they call the "tree"— every pass pattern in the playbook at full speed.

"It's having the will to be the best every day, every practice, every game," Harrison said. "I want to go out and get better, and I know Peyton is the same way."[5]

LIKE UNITAS AND BERRY

Their old-school work ethic reminds old-time NFL fans of great players from the past. Manning and Harrison have eclipsed another famous Colts tandem: quarterback Johnny Unitas and receiver Raymond Berry. They won NFL championships in 1958 and 1959 and were elected to the Hall of Fame.

"I was very young when Unitas and Berry were playing, but I would imagine it's pretty much the

DID YOU KNOW?

When salary cap dilemmas caused the Colts to consider roster changes following the 2005 season, the team opted to keep Marvin Harrison and allow Edgerrin James to leave as a free agent. The team believed Harrison's role in the Colts' offense was very important to Peyton Manning's success.

same thing," Coach Dungy said. "It doesn't happen much anymore because coaches change and move around in different systems, and players change. But they're very, very similar. It's a matter of trust."[6]

Manning shows how much he trusts Harrison every time he throws him the ball. In fact, Manning often throws a pass in Harrison's direction before the receiver makes his break. He trusts that his Pro Bowl receiver will be where he is supposed to be when the ball arrives. And he trusts that Harrison will catch almost every pass thrown his way.

"I feel like Marvin and I have put in a lot of work," Manning said. "We have put a lot of time and effort into it."[7]

With both Manning and Harrison under contract, the Colts expect the quarterback-receiver duo to increase their records and break even more for several years to come.

CHAPTER NINE

Playoff Winner

As Peyton Manning emerged as one of the
NFL's best quarterbacks, he continued to
face new challenges. The Colts were a team on the
rise, hungry to move among the league's elite. A
string of playoff losses early in his career, however,
threatened to distract from the achievements of the
Colts and their superstar quarterback.

Even the most successful quarterbacks are judged
by their records in playoff games. Many NFL Hall of
Fame quarterbacks, including John Elway, Roger
Staubach, and Steve Young, lost several playoff games
before finally winning the "Big One."

After the Colts' breakthrough season of 1999,
Manning led the Colts to five more winning seasons. But
critics said Manning had yet to arrive as the NFL's best
quarterback. They pointed to his lack of playoff wins.

Naysayers went back in time to build their case, pointing to the fact he never beat Florida during his four years at Tennessee. They also pointed out that his father, Archie, never made the playoffs in his fourteen years as an NFL quarterback.

Manning's father agonized over the undue criticism directed at his son. He knew that expectations come with the job, and he knew how unfair expectations could be.

"Gosh, I know how hard it is to succeed on that level, and trust me, it's just the worst thing to have to deal with," Archie Manning said.[1]

Instead of letting the playoff questions get to him, Manning chose to work harder at getting better and helping his team to win the next playoff game and to reach the ultimate goal: the Super Bowl.

Manning's improvement on the field was undeniable in the 2000 NFL season. He set team records for passing yards, completions, and 300-yard

"Don't try to define some-body's career in the middle of it. Let it play out and see what happens."

— Peyton Manning addressing his disappointing playoff record following an AFC Divisional Playoff loss to the Pittsburgh Steelers

DID YOU KNOW?

Unusual circumstances ended the No. 1-seeded Colts' trip to Peyton Manning's first Super Bowl. On January 15, 2006, in an AFC Divisional Playoff game against the Pittsburgh Steelers, Manning led the Colts to a last-minute comeback only to have their kicker miss a 46-yard field goal that would have tied the game.

games (5). He also passed for 33 touchdowns, breaking Johnny Unitas' Colts record of 32 in 1959.

The Colts' offense—still led by "The Triplets"—continued to thrive as Manning, James, and Harrison posted another 4,000–1,000–1,000 season.

Yet the team failed to repeat as division champions. They finished just one game behind Miami in a tough AFC East division. However, the Colts' 10–6 record qualified them for a wild-card playoff berth and a return game against the Dolphins.

Manning and the Colts jumped out to a 14–0 lead in the first half but struggled against a stout Miami defense in the second half. Manning completed just 17 of 32 pass attempts for 194 yards and one touchdown. But the Dolphins scored a game-tying touchdown late in the fourth quarter and won the game in overtime.

Manning passes during a losing effort against Buffalo in 2000.

The Colts had lost two straight playoff games by close margins, but neither Manning nor his teammates were ready to give up.

"Believe me," Manning said. "I want nothing more than to win a playoff game. But if we win our first-round game and get blown out in the second round, it's not like I'm going to put that high on my résumé."[2]

In 2001, Manning and the Colts suffered through a disappointing season. After winning their first two games by almost 40 points, the team lost three straight games, including two humiliating defeats at the hands of the New England Patriots. A five-game losing streak led to a 6–10 finish. The Colts were left out of the playoffs for the first time in two seasons.

Manning produced solid statistics, completing 62 percent of his passes for 4,131 yards and 26 touchdowns. An injury to James kept the offense from hitting on all cylinders.

UNDER NEW MANAGEMENT

As a result of the Colts' disappointing showing, Coach Jim Mora was fired after the season. He was replaced by Tony Dungy, who was known for building strong defenses.

Manning was glad the Colts hired Dungy. He knew the coach would let the team's high-powered offense stick with its game plan, while building a bigger, better defense in Indianapolis.

Dungy was a calm but strong presence in the locker room. His arrival helped the Colts put a losing season behind them and work toward returning to the playoffs in 2002.

As the season began, James continued to be hampered by injuries, putting extra pressure on the Colts' passing game. Manning took every snap for the third time of his career on the way to setting team single-season records for completions, attempts, and completion percentage.

He also became the only quarterback to throw for more than 4,000 passing yards in four consecutive seasons.

The Colts finished 10–6 and earned a wild-card playoff berth, giving Manning another chance to win his first NFL postseason game. Unfortunately, the New York Jets dominated the Colts 41–0. Manning completed just 14 of 31 pass attempts for 137 yards.

TAKING CARE OF THE LITTLE THINGS

After the game, Manning escaped to Mississippi. He spent several days alone in the woods. He hunted and

DID YOU KNOW?
The Colts' 2003 wild card game against the Jets was the first NFL playoff game to feature two African-American head coaches—Tony Dungy and Herm Edwards.

Manning and his coach, Tony Dungy

spent time thinking about the upcoming season.

"Believe me," he said, "I wish I could play a playoff game every week, because that's all people talk about: 'When is he gonna win a playoff game?' But the reality is, we've got sixteen regular season games to deal with first. If we can take care of the little things and get back to the postseason, I'll take my chances. Trust me—I'd rather be in the arena than be a guy who stops trying."[3]

"Pressure is something you feel only when you don't know what you're doing."

—Peyton Manning's favorite quote, coined by former Pittsburgh Steelers coach Chuck Noll

Manning and the Colts had returned to the playoffs but still had bad tastes in their mouths as they entered the 2004 season. Their playoff hopes immediately tasted sweeter when the Colts won the AFC's new South Division with a 12–4 record, their best since 1968.

Manning had a career season. He passed for more than 4,200 yards and 29 touchdowns. It was good enough to share the NFL's Most Valuable Player award with Tennessee quarterback Steve McNair.

As the Colts prepared for their opening playoff

game against Denver, Manning talked with confidence to Dungy, who had never won a playoff game as a head coach.

Manning and his coach were ready to shed the notion that they could not win a big game. When the game kicked off, the Colts unleashed all of their disappointment from past playoff failures on the Broncos.

The Colts left little doubt which team would advance, defeating Denver 41–10. Manning was incredible, completing 22 of 26 passes for 377 yards and 5 touchdowns. His 158.3 passer rating established a new Colts playoff record.

After the game, Dungy gave Manning credit for his first postseason win. He made a point to direct his comments at Manning's past critics.

"I hope people think this was a big game," Dungy said. "We kept hearing about Peyton's failure to win big games. I guess this was a big one."[4]

The following week, the Colts beat the Kansas City Chiefs for their second victory of the postseason, sending them to face the New England Patriots in the AFC Championship game.

Manning hands off to running back Edgerrin James.

The surprising Patriots, quarterbacked by Tom Brady, beat the Colts 24–14, preventing Manning from playing in his first Super Bowl. It was a sign of more disappointment to come for the Colts against the Patriots—and Brady against Manning.

The following season, Brady and the Patriots would knock the Colts out of the playoffs again, 20–3, causing some NFL critics to wonder if Brady was better suited than Manning to winning a championship.

"We wouldn't [trade Peyton] for what we do and I'm sure they wouldn't trade Brady for what they do," Dungy said.[5] Even with three Super Bowl titles to his credit, Brady recognized that Manning was a great quarterback to be reckoned with in 2005 and beyond.

"I love watching [Peyton] play and then you compete against him," Brady said. "Obviously the quarterbacks don't compete against each other, but as a team, you're competing against the team that he leads."[6]

Just as he had lifted the playoff jinx, Manning would later cast aside doubts that he couldn't beat Brady and the Patriots. Midway through the 2005 season, the Colts traveled to New England, where they had lost seven straight games against the Patriots.

Manning and the Colts made it clear they weren't going to suffer an eighth straight loss at New England. The Colts scored on seven of their first eight possessions, including 5 touchdowns on

New England quarterback Tom Brady chats with Manning.

the way to a 40–21 victory and finished with their highest scoring output in the franchise's 68-game history against the Patriots.

Manning scrambles during a game against the New England Patriots in Foxboro, Massachusetts, January 16, 2005.

Under a national spotlight, Manning was exceptional. He passed for 321 yards that included 2 touchdowns to Harrison and another to Reggie Wayne. James contributed 104 rushing yards and another touchdown.

The Colts' defense was as impressive as the offense, limiting Brady and the Patriots' offense to 102 total yards.

The Colts' 8–0 start in 2005 was a franchise best. Only 23 other NFL teams had ever survived their first eight games undefeated.

The win also proved that Manning was not going to stop until he quieted the critics and exceeded his goals for himself and the team.

CHAPTER TEN

PeyBack in Kindness

Being a professional athlete allows Peyton Manning to do more than play football. He and his family donate time and money to many charitable groups as part of the PeyBack Foundation.

Manning formed the PeyBack Foundation after his rookie season with the Colts as a way of giving back to the communities he grew to love during his football career.

Since 1999, the PeyBack Foundation has provided millions of dollars to programs that support its mission: to promote the future success of disadvantaged youth by providing leadership and growth opportunities for children at risk.

"I was blessed growing up in a loving, close-knit

family, which was made stronger by the presence of my dad, Archie," Manning said. "Now I want to give back to those kids who have been such terrific fans, but who may not have had the same sense of security and constant encouragement that I did as a child."[1]

The private, nonprofit corporation is a very important part of Manning's life as well as the lives of his family members. Several family members help him be a part of all major decisions that go into the foundation's annual programs. Manning serves as president, his wife, Ashley, is vice president, and his father, Archie, is secretary/treasurer.

One of the PeyBack Foundation's programs, Peyton's Pals, offers abused and neglected children monthly outings. On one outing, Manning took his pals on a trip to Disney World. Manning even surprised the graduates of the Peyton's Pals program with free laptop computers.

"It was neat to see their faces when they opened the boxes," Manning said. "These children have had to deal with a lot in a short amount of time. We knew how much a laptop would mean to them. The greatest joy for me and the Foundation was seeing

DID YOU KNOW?
Peyton Manning married his college sweetheart, Ashley Thompson, on March 17, 2001, in Memphis. She serves as an officer of the PeyBack Foundation.

Manning hugs Josh Schmitt, who played in the PeyBack Classic at the RCA Dome in Indianapolis September 23, 2005.

them smile at each event and leave here with new friends. That is our proudest accomplishment."[2]

After the presentation of the laptops, Manning shared his experience by offering the graduates advice for the future.

"I hope we have shown each of you the opportunities that exist for you as you get older," he told them. "I know life is tough on each of you. But you need to dream big and try to achieve your goals."[3]

The PeyBack Foundation also provides college scholarships to deserving students, organizes charity sports events, and donates money to youth football programs.

Football remains a big part of the foundation's work. The annual PeyBack Classic allows inner-city Indianapolis high school football teams to play in the RCA Dome and receive all the proceeds.

DID YOU KNOW?
Manning has been selected twice as the Walter Payton/Indianapolis Colts NFL Man of the Year for participation in community affairs. He also earned *USA Weekend's* Most Caring Athlete Award.

Through Manning's work with the National Football Foundation's Play It Smart campaign, the PeyBack Foundation helped place academic coaches at Indianapolis high schools.

Because Manning's time at the University of Tennessee was so important to his development as a person and a professional, his foundation's efforts also aid programs helping underprivileged children and the Boys & Girls Club in Tennessee.

HELPING AT HOME

The need for charity and aid recently hit closer to his home. After Hurricane Katrina's strong winds and heavy rains swept through New Orleans, the city suffered major flooding and extensive damage. Many thousands of people were left homeless, without even food or water.

Working with the PeyBack Foundation and the American Red Cross, Peyton Manning and his brothers helped load and unload an airliner with more than 30,000 pounds of supplies for the victims of Hurricane Katrina in their home state and city.

The sight of their flooded city and desperate neighbors was hard on the Manning brothers. They put their NFL celebrity aside as they handed out bottles of water, infant formula, diapers, and other necessities.

"The whole town is like family, so it's very much a personal issue," Manning said. "We grew up in New Orleans. We know these people; these people know us. We have a connection to these people."[4]

Archie and his sons also enjoy giving back to the game. The family devotes a portion of summer vacation to help young football players improve their offensive skills.

The Manning Passing Academy, a family-owned football camp held in Louisiana, creates an environment in which high school players can hone offensive fundamentals, techniques, and skills. Every summer, the Mannings enlist players and coaches from successful high school, college, and professional teams to help them teach at the academy.

Manning decided to start the camp after watching so many high school quarterbacks and teams struggle to throw the ball. As the camp's popularity grew, it began to attract players from across the country.

Manning points while working at the Manning Passing Academy in Hammond, Louisiana, July 10, 2004.

"It was really just going to be a regional thing," Manning said. "Now we have kids come from all over the country. And a lot of them come four straight years."[5]

The academy isn't limited to quarterbacks. Peyton, Cooper, Eli, and Archie Manning also offer drills and lessons designed for running backs, receivers, and tight ends.

The Mannings also make the time and effort to teach academy campers important lessons in motivation and sportsmanship.

"We get a lot of satisfaction from it," Archie said. "We try to teach the kids some good things, but we also have a lot of fun."[6]

CAREER STATISTICS

Year	Team	Games	Att.
1998	Colts	16	575
1999	Colts	16	533
2000	Colts	16	571
2001	Colts	16	547
2002	Colts	16	591
2003	Colts	16	566
2004	Colts	16	497
2005	Colts	16	453
Career		128	4,333

Comp.	Pct.	Yards	TDs	Int.
326	56.7	3,739	26	28
331	62.1	4,135	26	15
357	62.5	4,413	33	15
343	62.7	4,131	26	23
392	66.3	4,200	27	19
379	67.0	4,267	29	10
336	67.6	4,557	49	10
305	67.3	3,747	28	10
2,769	63.9	33,189	244	130

113

CAREER ACHIEVEMENTS

★ Set NFL single-season record with 49 touchdown passes in 2004

★ Named Associated Press NFL Most Valuable Player twice (2004 and sharing honors with Steve McNair in 2003)

★ Named to Associated Press NFL All-Pro First Teams twice (2003 and 2004)

★ Selected for the Pro Bowl six times (1999, 2000, 2002, 2003, 2004, 2005)

★ Named Most Valuable Player of 2004 Pro Bowl

★ Has completed better than 60 percent of his pass attempts in seven consecutive seasons following rookie season

★ Owns the longest career-opening streak of consecutive starts (128) of any NFL quarterback

★ Tied with Dan Marino for most games (6) with five or more touchdown passes

★ Named 2000 AFC Player of the Year

★ Set NFL and Colts rookie passing records for completions, attempts, and yards in 1998

★ First player chosen in the 1998 NFL Draft

★ Selected 1996 Southeastern Conference Player of the Year by The Associated Press

★ Named 1996 Sullivan Award winner as America's top amateur athlete

★ Winner of 1996 Maxwell Award as nation's most outstanding player

★ Only football player to have his jersey retired at the University of Tennessee

CHAPTER NOTES

CHAPTER 1. TOUCHDOWN KING

1. "Super Natural," *Sports Illustrated For Kids,* December 2005.

2. "Manning throws 6 TDs in less than three quarters," Associated Press, November 25, 2004, <http://sports.espn.go.com/nfl/recap?gameId=241125008> (November 15, 2005).

3. "Manning breaks record; Colts win in OT" *NFL.com* wire reports, December 26, 2004, <http://www.nfl.com/gamecenter/recap/NFL_20041226_SD@IND > (November 15, 2005).

4. "Manning throws 6 TDs in less than three quarters," Associated Press, November 25, 2004, <http://sports.espn.go.com/nfl/recap?gameId=241125008> (November 15, 2005).

CHAPTER 2. SON OF A QUARTERBACK

1. Archie and Peyton Manning with John Underwood, *Manning,* (Harper Entertainment, 2000) p. 15.

2. Ibid., p. 22.

3. Ibid., p. 40.

4. Ibid., p. 141.

5. Ibid., p. 96.

CHAPTER 3. BROTHER IN ARMS

1. Archie and Peyton Manning with John Underwood, *Manning,* (Harper Entertainment, 2000) p. 141.

2. "Peyton, Eli Give Brother Cooper A Fun Ride," *Nola.com*, December. 21, 2005, < http://www.nola.com/sports/t-p/index.ssf?/base/sports-21/1135148594129420.xml> (December 11, 2005).

3. Mark Stewart, *Peyton Manning: Rising Son*, (The Millbrook Press 2000) p. 7.

4. Archie and Peyton Manning with John Underwood, *Manning*, (Harper Entertainment, 2000) p. 199.

5. Ibid., p. 207.

CHAPTER 4. HIGH SCHOOL HOTSHOT

1. Archie and Peyton Manning with John Underwood, *Manning*, (Harper Entertainment, 2000) p. 199.

2. Ibid., p. 198.

3. Ibid., p. 222.

4. Ibid., p. 191.

5. Ibid., p. 191.

6. Ibid., p. 193.

CHAPTER 5. TENNESSEE VOLUNTEER

1. Archie and Peyton Manning with John Underwood, *Manning*, (Harper Entertainment, 2000) p. 242.

2. Mark Stewart, *Peyton Manning: Rising Son*, (The Millbrook Press 2000) p. 13.

3. "Plain and Simply Outstanding," *ESPN.com*, December 9, 2005, <http://sports.espn.go.com/espn/classic/bio/news/story?page=Manning_Peyton> (December 9, 2005).

4. Archie and Peyton Manning with John Underwood, *Manning*, (Harper Entertainment, 2000) p. 242.

5. Ibid., p. 246.

6. Jeff Savage, *Peyton Manning: Precision Passer*, (Lerner Sports, 2001) p. 36.

7. Ibid., p. 36.

8. Ibid., p. 38.

CHAPTER 6. NFL FRANCHISE ROOKIE

1. Archie and Peyton Manning with John Underwood, *Manning*, (Harper Entertainment, 2000) p. 294.

2. Mark Stewart, *Peyton Manning: Rising Son*, (The Millbrook Press 2000) p. 32.

3. Ibid., p. 36.

4. Archie and Peyton Manning with John Underwood, *Manning*, (Harper Entertainment, 2000) p. 332.

5. "Super Natural," *Sports Illustrated For Kids,* December 2005.

6. Ibid.

7. Ibid.

8. Jeff Savage, *Peyton Manning: Precision Passer*, (Lerner Sports, 2001) p. 48.

CHAPTER 7. BREAKTHROUGH SEASON

1. Archie and Peyton Manning with John Underwood, *Manning*, (Harper Entertainment, 2000) p. 349.

2. Jeff Savage, *Peyton Manning: Precision Passer*, (Lerner Sports 2001) p. 49.

3. Archie and Peyton Manning with John Underwood, *Manning*, (Harper Entertainment, 2000) p. 252.

4. Jeff Savage, *Peyton Manning: Precision Passer*, (Lerner Sports 2001) p. 51.

CHAPTER 8. MANNING AND HARRISON

1. "Making History," *Colts.com*, October 18, 2005, <http://www.colts. com/sub.cfm?page=article7&news_id=3204> (December 18, 2005).

2. "Manning, Harrison duo 2nd to none in NFL," *msnbc.com*, September 2, 2004, <http://www.msnbc.msn.com/id/5876762/from/RL.4/> (December 18, 2005).

3. "Manning, Harrison breaking all the records," *msnbc.com*, Sept. 15, 2005, <http://www.msnbc.msn.com/id/9357132/from/RL.2/> (December 18, 2005).

4. "Perfect together," *nydailynews.com*, September 7, 2005, <www.nydai-lynews.com/sports/football/story/344219p-293901c.html> (December 10, 2005).

5. Ibid.

6. "Super Natural," *Sports Illustrated For Kids*, December 2005.

7. "Making History," *Colts.com*, October 18, 2005, <http://www.colts.com/ sub.cfm?page=article7&news_id=3204> (December 10, 2005).

CHAPTER 9. PLAYOFF WINNER

1. "Pressure's on Peyton," *si.com*, January 9, 2004, <http://sportsillus-trated.cnn.com/2004/writers/michael_silver/01/09/open_mike/index.ht ml> (December 7, 2005).

2. Ibid.

3. Ibid.

4. "Manning dominant in first playoff win," *NFL.com*, January 4, 2004,< http://www.nfl.com/gamecenter/recap/NFL_20040104_DEN@IND>.

5. "Aces face to face," *Indystar.com*, November 7, 2005, <http://www.indystar.com/apps/pbcs.dll/article?AID=/20051107/SPORT S03/511070370/1004/SPORTS> (December 5, 2005).

6. Ibid.

CHAPTER 10. PEYBACK IN KINDNESS

1. "Letter From Peyton," *peytonmanning.com*, <http://www.peytonman-ning.com/peyback/foundation/letter.cfm> (December 27, 2005).

2. "Peyton's Pals Ends First Year with Surprise from Peyton," *peytonman-ning.com*, March 4, 2005, < http://www.peytonmanning.com/newsroom/newsreleases/030705.cfm> (December 15, 2005).

3. Ibid.

4. "Manning brothers team up for Katrina relief," *cnn.com*, September 5, 2005, < http://www.cnn.com/2005/US/09/04/mannings.relief/> (December 14, 2005).

5. "Mannings pass knowledge to eager youths," *NFL.com*, July 11, 2003, <http://www.nfl.com/news/story/6476152 > (December 8, 2005).

6. Ibid.

GLOSSARY

American Football Conference (AFC)—One of two conferences of National Football League teams.

cut—To suddenly change direction to lose a pursuing player.

defense—The team defending its goal line. The defense does not have the ball; rather, they attempt to keep the offense from passing or running the ball over their (the defense's) goal line.

draft—The selection of new players into the pro ranks. Teams doing poorly are allowed to choose before those doing well. Teams pick from among the various top college players.

fullback—A member of the offense whose job it is to block for the halfback and quarterback, but he also runs the ball and receives passes. The name comes from the fact the fullback lines up the farthest behind the quarterback.

letterman—A high school or college athlete who participates in enough plays to earn a letter jacket.

linebacker—Defensive players placed behind the defensive linemen. Their job is to tackle runners and block or intercept passes. There are three or four linebackers in a starting lineup.

National Football Conference (NFC)—One of two conferences of National Football League teams.

National Football League (NFL)—The best-known association of professional football teams. It is composed of the American Football and National Football conferences, which each have 16 teams.

offense—The team with the ball. The offense attempts to run or pass the ball across the defense's goal line.

offensive backfield—The area or players behind the offensive linemen. These are the running backs and the quarterback.

passer rating—Combination of NFL statistics designed to rate a quarterback's performance.

playbook—A notebook containing a team's terms, strategies, plays, etc., issued to each player.

playoffs—A series of postseason games leading to the Super Bowl.

Pro Bowl—NFL players, coaches, and fans select the season's best players in the AFC and the NFC to play in this all-star game in Hawaii a week after the Super Bowl.

quarterback—The leader of the offense. The quarterback calls plays and receives the snap from the center to begin each play. He can hand off or pass the ball to another player or run the ball himself.

quarterback sack—When a defensive player tackles the quarterback before he can pass the ball.

receiver—An offensive player whose main job is catching passes.

regular season—A time period of seventeen weeks during which a team plays sixteen games to determine its ranking going into the playoffs.

running back—Positioned behind the quarterback, there are two running backs. Their job is to run with the ball, which is typically handed off by the quarterback. They are part of the offensive backfield. In college and high school football, there are halfbacks and fullbacks in these positions, but in professional football there are simply the two running backs.

rush—To run from the line of scrimmage with the ball.

Super Bowl—The NFL's championship game pitting the winner of the AFC versus the winner of the NFC.

tight end—An offensive player who usually lines up next to the offensive linemen. Sometimes his job is to help the linemen block on running plays. Other times, the tight end goes out to catch passes, like a receiver.

FOR MORE INFORMATION

FURTHER READING

Manning, Archie, and Peyton Manning with John Underwood. *Manning*. Harper Entertainment, 2000.

Polzer, Tim *Quarterback Power*. Scholastic, 2004.

Savage, Jeff. *Peyton Manning: Precision Passer*. Lerner Sports, 2001.

Stewart, Mark. *Peyton Manning: Rising Son*. The Millbrook Press, 2000.

WEB LINKS

Manning's *NFL.com* page
http://www.nfl.com/players/playerpage/12531

Manning's Web site
http://www.peytonmanning.com

The Manning Passing Academy site
http://www.manningpassingacademy.com/

Manning's page on *Colts.com*
http://www.colts.com/sub.cfm?page=bio&player_id=8

Indianapolis Colts' site
http://www.colts.com

Tennessee Athletics
http://utsports.collegesports.com/

INDEX

E

K

Kansas City Chiefs, 12, 14, 83, 100

Kearse, Jevon, 82

L

Leaf, Ryan, 63, 65, 71, 78

M

Manning, Archie, 16–17, 19–26, 27–28, 30–31, 33, 34, 35, 38, 40, 41, 48, 66, 93, 107, 110, 111

Manning, Ashley (Thompson), 54, 107

Manning, Cooper, 16, 23, 24, 27–28, 30–31, 33, 34–35, 36, 39, 40, 41, 42, 44–45, 46–48, 111

Manning, Eli, 16, 20, 23, 27, 28, 30, 31, 36–38, 111

Manning, Olivia, 20, 21, 23, 24, 26, 31, 33, 34, 41

Manning Passing Academy, 110–111

Manning, Peyton

becomes Colts' starting quarterback, 69

birth of, 16

choosing University of Tennessee, 49

growing up, 19, 23–25, 27–28, 30–31, 33–37

at Isidore Newman School, 40–42, 44–46

jersey retired, 62

named All–American, 46, 62

named MVP, 46, 99

wins Sullivan Award, 62

Marino, Dan, 7, 8, 9–10, 11–12, 13, 14, 70

McNair, Steve, 99

Miami Dolphins, 8, 9, 69–70, 78, 83, 94